# MID-NOVEL REVISION PROMPTS:

## INSPIRING IDEAS FOR YOUR BOOK-IN-PROGRESS

by Rayne Hall

**MID-NOVEL REVISION PROMPTS: INSPIRING IDEAS FOR YOUR BOOK-IN-PROGRESS**

by Rayne Hall

Book cover by Erica Syverson and Uros Jovanovic

March 2017 Edition

ISBN-13: 978-1543190410

British English.

# INTRODUCTION

Do you want a daily dose of inspiration to carry your novel plot forward? Conventional lists of writing prompts are great for starting new projects, but don't work if you're already well into a story with developed characters and an ongoing plot. This book can help.

Whether you seek to boost your own imagination, to rekindle your passion for a book project or to release a creative block, these prompts will get the juices flowing.

Did you know that human creativity performs best under pressure, when it has a specific problem to solve? Given unlimited time and freedom, many a writer's imagination dries up. With an assignment and a deadline, however, creativity flourishes.

The writing prompts in this book deliver this challenge. If you ask your brain to come up with solutions fast, it will respond to the pressure. Give your brain a task and the freedom as to how to solve it, and you'll stimulate original ideas and high productivity.

For best effect, pick a prompt at random, or ask a friend to give you a number between one and 100, and stick with that choice. Don't allow yourself to browse until you find the ideal prompt, because this would remove the challenge factor. You may, however, amend the prompt (for example, changing the gender of the characters) and interpret it freely, so that it suits your genre and plot.

Set a kitchen timer or countdown clock to ten minutes. Freewrite about the topic—preferably in longhand on paper—jotting down ideas how this scenario might play out in your novel. Write fast without pausing, and don't censor your thoughts. When the ten minutes are up, take a quick break, and perhaps drink some coffee or water, before you look at your notes.

Underline anything usable, play with the ideas you've come up with, and plan how to build them into the scene. Then get writing.

This method works well whether you're doing it on your own or with writing buddies. Several of you can meet up, perhaps over a latte in your favourite coffee shop. One picks the prompt, and everyone responds to it. At the end of the 10-minute freewrite, you can discuss your ideas. This ensures you're all honouring the prompts and you won't be tempted to cheat. Shared writing sessions are great for NaNoWriMo (National Novel Writing Month) participants and writers' circles.

To stimulate the flow of your imagination, I provide some ideas for every prompt: guiding questions, what-if scenarios, and suggestions for how you might interpret the topic. While they may not be an exact fit for your novel, they will open the floodgates so your own ideas gush forth.

Once you've used a prompt, highlight it or write it in a list. Although you can use the same prompt twice, fresh prompts are more fun.

Please note: this is not a novel-plotting guide. If you want structural help for your 'sagging middle', you may find my book *Writing Vivid Plots* more useful.

I've written the prompts in British English, with British grammar, vocabulary, punctuation and spelling. You can change them to American (or other regional) English.

'MC' stands for 'main character', the hero/protagonist of your book.

Are you ready to start? Set the timer. Ten minutes. Go!

Rayne Hall

# MID-NOVEL WRITING PROMPT
## #1

*The MC's secret is in danger of being discovered or exposed. What does he do to preserve his secret?*

**Ideas you can use:**

Is it his own secret, or is he covering for someone else?

Is this a secret he only needs to guard for a short time, or something that affects his whole life?

Will all be well if he manages to protect the secret in this scene, or does the whole novel revolve around it?

What would happen if the truth was found out? What would be the terrible consequences—for the MC or for someone else?

Who nearly discovers (or who almost exposes) the secret? How?

How does the MC feel at the moment of almost-exposure?

What does the MC do to protect the secret? Does he change the subject, deny the fact, ridicule the speaker, or...?

Perhaps the MC manages to preserve the secret in this scene... but to do this, he has to weave additional lies, which will cause problems for him later on.

# MID-NOVEL WRITING PROMPT
## #2

*An animal plays an active role in this scene. What does it want and do?*

**Ideas you can use:**

What kind of animal might fit into the story at this stage? A pet or a working animal? Perhaps a cat or dog? What about a carrier pigeon, a load-carrying mule, a carthorse? Might it be a riding animal such as a camel, donkey, horse or elephant? What about a curious animal, perhaps a cheeky robin or monkey wanting to see what's going on?

Perhaps the animal is dangerous. What if the characters encounter a cobra, a tiger, a rabies-infected fox?

Maybe the animal is injured and needs help. Will and can the MC help?

What if the animal is hungry and approaches the humans, begging for food? What if the ravenous animal views humans as food?

Maybe the animal causes problems by its presence—giving away the character's hiding place, or distracting her by demanding cuddles when she needs to concentrate on a difficult task.

What kind of animal do you understand really well? If this species suits the story, you can write about it with convincing authenticity.

How about an unusual pet? A character might keep a crow, rat or lizard.

What about a magician's familiar?

# MID-NOVEL WRITING PROMPT
## #3

*Two of the MC's deeply-held loyalties are in conflict. How?*

**Ideas you can use:**

What if he owes loyalty to two people—and they make incompatible demands? His liege lord and his betrothed, perhaps? Or his wife and his mother? His employer and his friend?

What if the loyalty is to organisations, causes, nations? Perhaps he is loyal to the company that employs him—but also to a campaign to protect the environment, and he discovers that the factory is leaking toxic substances into the groundwater. What if he is a military officer, seconded to an allied power, has made friends there and raised a family—and now the political landscape has changed, the former allies are enemies, and he gets recalled and must destroy the people he loves?

What if he is loyal to two people, and one of them is present to make demands, while the other is not even aware of the conflict?

How does the MC respond to this inner conflict? Does he immediately realise the dilemma, or does it dawn on him only later—when he has already committed himself to one cause? Does he try to gain time, does he placate both sides, does he make promises he can't keep, or does he try to stay out of it? Does he ask someone for advice? Whom?

How does this inner conflict feel physically? Does it give him a headache, a sinking sensation in the stomach, or a tightness in the chest?

# MID-NOVEL WRITING PROMPT
## #4

*The weather becomes extreme. How do the characters react?*

**Ideas you can use:**

What kind of extreme weather is common in the region where your novel takes place? What kind of extreme weather is rare, but just plausible?

Could the next scene feature freezing cold, a heatwave, a hurricane, a hail storm or a monsoon?

How do the characters react to the weather?

Are they prepared for this weather?

How does the weather affect their actions, their plans, their moods?

# MID-NOVEL WRITING PROMPT
## #5

*The MC counts on someone's support—but that person has her own agenda.*

**Ideas you can use:**

What kind of support does the MC need in the coming scene? From whom? Why does he expect to get it?

Why does the other person not give the support required? Perhaps she has a previous commitment to someone else, or conscientious objections? Or maybe she simply doesn't like to shoulder the work or expense involved?

What if the person agrees to provide the requested support—but on a condition. "I'll do this for you, but only if you do that for me." Is that condition acceptable?

What if the person blackmails the MC? "Unless you pay me this exorbitant amount/give me a glowing job reference/pass me in the exam, I won't do what you so desperately need."

What if the person agrees to the support but backs out at the last minute, or without notifying the MC that he won't be there?

# MID-NOVEL WRITING PROMPT
# #6

## *The MC helps a vulnerable person.*

**Ideas you can use:**

In what way is that person vulnerable? Is he poor, sick, frail, elderly, injured? Does he belong to an ethnic minority or a lower class? Does his appearance, religion or personality mark him as a victim for bullies?

How does the MC help? Does she give him money, a care parcel of food, advice or encouragement? Does she defend him against verbal bullying or physical abuse?

Does she give this help openly or in secret? Does she help casually as a matter of course without thinking about it, simply because she's kind and compassionate, or pointedly, to show others what she thinks of their refusal to help? Perhaps she does it as a public relations measure, to demonstrate publicly what a good person she is?

Is the person she helps a character in the novel whom the reader already knows and will meet again—or someone seen only this once?

Does the MC fully understand what she is doing? Do her actions have repercussions later in the novel? What if the man she helps is one of the evil villain's minions? What if his suffering is punishment by a cruel warlord who does not tolerate meddling?

# MID-NOVEL WRITING PROMPT
## #7

*The MC needs to leave the room/building/vehicle but can't get out.*

**Ideas you can use:**

Why does he need to get out? To go to an appointment, to fetch food, to use the toilet, to escape from an assassin, to get an urgent message to someone?

Why can't he leave? Because everyone in the room is watching him, so he can't sneak out unobserved? Or because he's been locked in? Maybe the lock is jammed? Perhaps the car is stuck in a snowdrift? What if a high-ranking or important personage keeps talking to the MC, and he doesn't want to offend her?

# MID-NOVEL WRITING PROMPT
## #8

*A problem with the building or location causes discomfort or disruption.*

**Ideas you can use:**

What could happen if the scene takes place indoors? How about a burst waterpipe, a collapsing roof, a power cut, a heater that doesn't work?

For an outdoor scene, maybe the location is flooded or frozen. Perhaps a fierce wind makes the conversation inaudible, a fallen tree blocks the road, or a sudden downpour drenches everyone?

# MID-NOVEL WRITING PROMPT
## #9

*The MC accidentally stumbles across someone's secret.*

**Ideas you can use:**

Whose secret is it? Why does this character hide it? How does the MC discover it?

How does the MC feel about the secret? How does the secret affect his opinion of that person?

What does he do about the discovery? Does he ignore it or does he tell the secret-keeper? Does he help to protect the secret, or will he make it public? What if he sees an opportunity for blackmail or revenge?

# MID-NOVEL WRITING PROMPT
## #10

*The MC learns something which makes him suspicious of someone he has always trusted.*

**Ideas you can use:**

Of whom does he become suspicious? Someone he thought was a loyal ally, or a personage he thought was neutral?

What causes the suspicion? Does it arise suddenly or gradually?

Should the suspicion turn out to be correct, how will it affect the MC's plans? How will it affect other people?

What does the MC do about it? Hide the suspicion and act as if everything was as before? Confront the person? Share the suspicion with a close friend to get a second opinion?

Should the suspicion turn out to be false, what consequences might a false accusation have for the MC?

# MID-NOVEL WRITING PROMPT
## #11

*An overheard snippet of conversation turns the MC's perceptions upside down.*

**Ideas you can use:**

What is that overheard comment about, and in what way does it change her perceptions? Are people discussing an event they'd attended, and their version is different from what she had been told? Is she a homicide investigator, and discovers that the main witness could not have seen anything because he was somewhere else that day? What if it dawns on her that the child protection charity to which she has devoted all her time and resources is really a cover for child trafficking? What if she learns something shocking about the man with whom she's in love? What if she discovers that her fiancé already has a wife?

How does she come to hear it? Where does this take place? Perhaps she's in a bus, and the people on the seat behind her are talking. She could also overhear chats in a coffee shop, in a dentist's waiting room or in a supermarket queue.

Does she immediately realise the importance of what she has heard, or does the comment niggle at her for a long time? Perhaps she dismisses it at first, assuming the speaker must be mistaken, or she must have misheard, because she is certain that her view is right.

Maybe she doesn't grasp the significance at first, and when she decides she needs to verify the statement and find out more, the strangers have already left the bus.

# MID-NOVEL WRITING PROMPT
## #12

*A character gets injured.*

**Ideas you can use:**

What if the MC sustains an injury that prevents him from pursuing his goal the way he had planned? What will he do now?

What if an important team member can't join the expedition or has to drop out of the project because of the injury? How can they continue without him?

What if it's the MC's enemy who gets hurt? Will the MC take advantage, or help him, or pretend he did not notice?

What caused the injury? A thug attack, a duel, an ambitious sporting venture, a misstep during a daring escape?

How does it affect the character? Does the injury slow him, restrict what he can do, or put him out of action completely for a while?

# MID-NOVEL WRITING PROMPT
## #13

*A message arrives in an unusual way.*

**Ideas you can use:**

How does it arrive? By carrier pigeon? As a message in a bottle? Scribbled inside a cornflakes box? Spelled out on a Ouija board? In a dream? A lady tapping it in Morse code with her high heels on the floor?

Does the recipient expect a message or find it by accident?

Does she read it openly, or hide it from other people?

What if the person who finds the message is not the one for whom it was intended?

What effect does the message have on the recipient? Does she take action, change her plans, or laugh the whole thing off?

# MID-NOVEL WRITING PROMPT
## #14

### *The MC loses an important ally.*

**Ideas you can use**

What happens? Does the ally desert the cause, perhaps even defect to the enemy? Does he betray the MC, maybe revealing her trade secrets or personal weaknesses to the competitor? Maybe he simply isn't there where she needs him, because he doesn't consider her cause to be as important as watching the football match on TV.

Perhaps he never really was an ally, but an agent in the enemy's employ who infiltrated the MC's circle?

What if the loyal ally dies? Perhaps the evil overlord sent an assassin, or maybe the ally sacrificed his life for the MC or the noble cause.

The loss—whether by defection, betrayal or death—hurts. What is the MC's emotional reaction? What actions does she take immediately? How does she change her long-term plans?

# MID-NOVEL WRITING PROMPT
## #15

*The MC realises that she was wrong.*

**Ideas you can use:**

About what was she wrong? For how long has she clung to that mistaken belief?

What causes her to change her mind? Was this a result of rational analysis, or did her conscience make her reconsider? Does a conversation with a trusted friend or spiritual advisor open up a new perspective? Does she see with her own eyes the terrible effects of the method she had supported? Does she discover a new fact, or evidence that was previously hidden?

# MID-NOVEL WRITING PROMPT
## #16

*Something requires more effort than expected.*

**Ideas you can use:**

What is it the MC tries to do in this scene? It can be his main scene goal, e.g. persuade his aunt to lend him the money, or it can be a contributing action, e.g. fix his aunt's car.

Is he scaling a cliff, retrieving a wallet from the bottom of the fish pond, digging an escape tunnel, building a model aeroplane, cooking the perfect dinner for twelve, or navigating by car in an unfamiliar city?

How does the MC respond to the difficulty? Does he simply work harder, or does he try a different approach? Perhaps he borrows a tool from the neighbour, or asks the neighbour to lend a hand.

Maybe it's not the MC, but another character struggling with the effort. What if the MC witnesses how his aunt tries to fix the car herself?

What if a team labours over a task, and it requires more effort than expected? Is everyone pulling their weight? If not, do tensions arise?

# MID-NOVEL WRITING PROMPT
## #17

*A character discovers an object from the past.*

**Ideas you can use:**

What is it? A photo, a drawing, a valuable heirloom, a letter, a written confession, an amateur video, an ancient coin, a treasure map?

What does he do with it? To whom does he show it? In what way does this item influence the character's actions in this scene? Does it play a role later in the story?

# MID-NOVEL WRITING PROMPT
## #18

*An action requires physical strength.*

**Ideas you can use:**

What is the action? Pushing a car, lifting a heavy suitcase, digging a garden bed, pulling a sledge, climbing a mountain, carrying bricks, breaking down a locked door, training a horse?

Who is doing this—the MC or one of the other characters? Does it involve several people?

Is she strong enough to accomplish the task? Did she expect to need that much strength? Can she ask for help—her husband, her flatmate, her neighbour? Will they help?

Is she using a tool such as a lever or rollers, or does she depend on her body strength alone?

# MID-NOVEL WRITING PROMPT
## #19

*The scene takes place in a dangerous location.*

**Ideas you can use:**

If you initially envisaged the scene in a safe environment, consider moving it to a more dangerous place, or introducing an element of danger to the current location.

If your characters are climbing a mountain, might the rock face be unstable or crumbling? If they're bathing in the sea, could there be reports of shark sightings in that bay? If they're strolling in the country park, might the path have disappeared in a recent landslide, forcing them to walk across boulders and debris? What if they're walking along the seashore—might a steep cliff tower above them, with warning signs "unstable cliff surface—keep clear" while the high tide comes rolling in?

The courting couple may enjoy a picnic in the forest clearing, but they know there are wolves in these woods so they won't completely relax.

The challenge is greater for an indoor scene. If the characters meet in the restaurant, they may worry about the rough, brutal-looking characters at the other tables, and the evidence of recent violence. Perhaps the house stands in an earthquake zone, when another big one is predicted, and every rumbling noise puts them on high alert.

If they're in a car, perhaps the road on which they're travelling is slippery with black ice, or consists of one hairline curve after another, with no barrier separating the narrow road from the sheer drop.

How do the characters react to the danger? Have they taken safety precautions or do they deny that there is a risk? Do they joke about the dangers, or jump every time they hear what might be a wolf's howl or a distant tremor?

# MID-NOVEL WRITING PROMPT
## #20

*The MC is hungry or thirsty, but unable to get food or drink.*

**Ideas you can use:**

Why can't he get food or drink? What if he is in a remote location, with no human settlement nearby? What if he's on an expedition, and his provisions have been lost? Perhaps he doesn't have the money to buy food, and is too embarrassed to ask others for help. Maybe he's locked up in a prison cell, with only minute rations of bread and water. Or perhaps an enemy has left him to die from starvation. What if the castle is under siege, or a war is on, and the inhabitants have to survive on smaller and smaller rations?

What does he do cope with his body's cravings? Scavenge, steal, hunt rats, chew grass, tighten the belt around his waist, distract himself, pray for help, or meditate to transcend beyond bodily cravings?

How does the hunger or thirst feel physically? Describe them so vividly that the readers get hungry or thirsty. Is the hunger or thirst getting worse throughout the scene?

# MID-NOVEL WRITING PROMPT
## #21

*The MC doesn't want to tell a lie, but speaking the truth will get someone else into trouble.*

**Ideas you can use:**

This is probably a dialogue scene, in which one character asks questions, and the MC evades. Why is he protecting the other person—out of loyalty, from compassion, or because of a promise?

In what way would that person get into trouble?

Who is probing—a friend, a family member, an employer or a police officer? What does the questioner believe really happened?

What does the MC do to wiggle out of the situation—try to change the subject, asking questions back, verbally attack the questioner, invent an excuse to get away?

# MID-NOVEL WRITING PROMPT
## #22

*Something the MC did at the beginning of the novel now causes him serious trouble.*

**Ideas you can use:**

Did the MC make a bad decision? Did he tell a lie that is now difficult to maintain? Did he fall in with the wrong company? Did he insult a person who turns out to be a powerful enemy? Did he commit a crime that's been found out? Did he betray someone whose help he now desperately needs?

# MID-NOVEL WRITING PROMPT
## #23

*Someone turns up unexpectedly—and it's not someone the MC wants to see right now.*

**Ideas you can use:**

Who is this unexpected arrival—and why does the MC not want to see him? Perhaps an ex-boyfriend turns up while she's enjoying a hot date with a new man? What if it's the husband she claimed (or believed) died years ago? How about a love rival who joins their table just when she thinks she has enchanted the man? Perhaps she has just promised her boss that her family will never again interfere with her job duties—and her teenage son turns up that moment, demanding that she must come home at once. What if a police officer arrives while she is hiding the evidence? Or perhaps it's the bailiff, or the landlord, or the loan shark with a final demand?

A less dramatic situation is also possible. Maybe the new arrival is simply someone obnoxious or irritating who demands attention while she needs to concentrate on an important task.

# MID-NOVEL WRITING PROMPT
## #24

*A signpost, warning sign or poster inspires the MC to change her plans.*

**Ideas you can use:**

What had she planned? What will she do instead?

Where is this signpost, warning sign or poster? On a wall in a restaurant, at a crossroads or fork in the road, in a railway carriage, at a bus stop? What does it say?

Does she heed the warning or take up the suggestion? Or does she do the opposite of what the sign says?

What if it's not the written statement that affects the MC? Maybe one of the words triggers a memory, and she changes her plans because of what she suddenly remembers.

# MID-NOVEL WRITING PROMPT
## #25

*A power cut or fuel shortage causes complications or discomfort.*

**Ideas you can use:**

What kind of power or fuel would the characters use in this situation? Wood? Coal? Petroleum? Gas? Electricity?

Is it running low for these specific people only, or is there a regional or nationwide shortage?

What causes this shortage? Perhaps fuel has been rationed because of the war. Maybe the MC hasn't paid his bills, and the supplier has turned off the gas and electricity. Has a worldwide oil shortage all but stopped private cars? Maybe the wood the characters gathered for their campfire has all burned. What if one character was supposed to provide the fuel, but forgot?

# MID-NOVEL WRITING PROMPT
## #26

### *The location is dark.*

**Ideas you can use:**

How about a cave, an unlit cellar, a cinema, a dark alleyway at night? Or perhaps the scene could play out in a dingy pub, a seedy nightclub, or in the home of people who can't afford electricity for lighting.

What if the characters operate in the dark because they don't want to use lights to avoid discovery?

# MID-NOVEL WRITING PROMPT
## #27

*Describe the ground or floor of the current location in a way that gives the reader a clear idea of the place.*

**Ideas you can use:**

Does the scene take place indoors? Then show the deep-pile rugs, the valuable Persian carpet, the hardwood flooring, the woven ethnic throws, the threadbare wall-to-wall carpet, the splintered wooden steps, the scuffed linoleum. How clean or dirty is the floor? Is it stained (if yes, what kind of stains?), covered in crumbs or debris (if yes, what kind?) or polished to a high sheen?

For an outdoor location, show the black chewing gum and white seagull droppings splotching the asphalt, the meticulously manicured lawn, the weeds between the mossed-over paving slabs, the gravel that crunches under the steps, the crumbling pavement (American: sidewalk), the oil spills on the tarmac, the yellowing grasses in the drought-stricken park.

As well as describing the ground visually, consider using at least one other sense. For example, describe the sounds of footsteps on the floor, or how the ground feels underfoot.

# MID-NOVEL WRITING PROMPT
## #28

*The MC needs a favour from someone who doesn't mean to grant it.*

**Ideas you can use:**

What kind of favour does the MC need? From whom?

Does he expect to get it? Why? Because the other person owes him a favour? Or because it's such a simple or honourable thing, no right-minded person would refuse?

Why does the other character decline? Does she have personal reasons, or is she simply mean? What if she wants to teach the MC a lesson? What if she is practising extortion, perhaps by demanding payment or a return favour that the MC doesn't want to grant?

# MID-NOVEL WRITING PROMPT
## #29

*A meeting takes place in a different location than expected.*

**Ideas you can use:**

Why is the original meeting place not available? Perhaps the bar is closed, the house flattened by an earthquake, the factory staked out by police, the crime scene cordoned off?

Where do the characters meet instead? In what way does the new location change the mood of the meeting or affect its outcome?

# MID-NOVEL WRITING PROMPT
## #30

*The MC witnesses or participates in a ritual.*

**Ideas you can use:**

The ritual could be religious or spiritual. It may be a family tradition, or a native custom, or an annual local event.

It may be something small—such as a libation offered to the household gods before a meal—or a lengthy procedure spanning the duration of the scene.

Is the MC experiencing this for the first time, or is it something he's grown up with?

How does he feel about it?

# MID-NOVEL WRITING PROMPT
## #31

*The MC can't find the item she needs.*

**Ideas you can use:**

What is she looking for? Her passport, her marriage certificate, her house key, the evidence for a crime?

Where is she looking for them?

What happens if she doesn't find the item? Does she worry, panic or laugh? Does she feel angry, frightened, stressed, suspicious, impatient?

If she finds the item eventually, what are the consequences of the delay? Does the search for her house key mean the killer catches up with her on the doorstep? While she's searching for her driving licence, does the police officer notice the blood stains on the back seat?

If the item has vanished for good, what does this mean for her and for the plot? Perhaps the loss is a drastic setback for her pursuit of her big goal.

# MID-NOVEL WRITING PROMPT
## #32

*A friend acts out of character.*

**Ideas you can use:**

Who is that friend? What behaviour would be normal for him in this situation?

In what way does he act differently? What causes his behaviour?

Who notices?

# MID-NOVEL WRITING PROMPT
## #33

*A character is dressed wrongly for the weather or the occasion.*

**Ideas you can use:**

Who is dressed wrongly—the MC or another character?

What would be the normal choice of dress?

In what way is this character's dress not appropriate? Is it too formal for a casual occasion, too expensive for a charity visit to the slums, too tight-fitting for vigorous activity, too garish for a funeral? Maybe she's wearing high heels to walk on an icy road, a sleeveless dress in the snow, or a thick jacket in the sweltering heat. Perhaps she's arrived at a theatre gala in jeans, when all the other ladies wear evening gowns and tiaras. Or maybe she's the one in decked out in sequins and tiaras when everyone else wears denim casuals.

Is the character aware of the inappropriate dress? If yes, how does she feel about it? Mortified with embarrassment, or indifferent to what other people think?

Why is she dressed wrongly? Did she not have time to get changed after work? Is she away from home, with limited luggage? What if she has escaped from the villain's clutches in the clothes she was wearing? Or perhaps she simply trusted the weather forecast.

# MID-NOVEL WRITING PROMPT
## #34

*A vehicle or appliance breaks down just when it's needed most.*

**Ideas you can use:**

What breaks down—the escape vehicle, the heating, the sound system? What if the computer crashes at the worst possible moment, or the mobile phone (American: cell phone) battery is empty?

Why would it be needed so much? The breakdown probably delays an urgent action. What is this urgent action?

How does the character cope without the device?

# MID-NOVEL WRITING PROMPT
## #35

*A secret can no longer be kept.*

**Ideas you can use:**

What is the secret? Who is keeping it—the MC or another character?

What has changed to force the character to come clean? Is he under suspicion for a crime, or do his peers exert pressure? Has he tangled himself in a net of lies so nobody believes him anymore?

# MID-NOVEL WRITING PROMPT
## #36

*A character arrives late to an important appointment, meeting or event.*

**Ideas you can use:**

What is this event? Who is present?

Who is late—the MC or another character?

Why is he late? Did he lose the way or remember the appointment only just in time? Was he held up by an emergency at work, did the babysitter let him down, or did he have an accident? Perhaps he is simply the kind of guy who doesn't think punctuality important.

How do the other characters react? Have they started the meeting without him? Do they ignore this late arrival, or reprimand him?

How does he excuse his lateness? Does he apologise? Does he give a reason? Does he simply sit down and act as if his lateness didn't matter?

In what way does his late arrival cause problems for him, for others, or for the plot?

# MID-NOVEL WRITING PROMPT
## #37

*A character confesses/reveals something the other person would rather not know.*

**Ideas you can use:**

Who confesses what to whom? Why does he confess now?

Why would the other person rather not know? Does she try to stop the confession? If yes, how? Does she ask him to stop, does she change the subject, does she pretend not to listen?

What does this knowledge mean to the recipient? In what way does the confession affect the plot?

# MID-NOVEL WRITING PROMPT
## #38

*A character needs a skill she neglected to learn.*

**Ideas you can use:**

Who is the character—the MC or someone else?

What skill would she find really useful right now? Speaking German, picking locks, cooking omelettes, playing chess, changing a car tyre?

When did she have the opportunity to learn this skill: earlier in the novel or earlier in her life? Why did she choose not to learn it?

# MID-NOVEL WRITING PROMPT
## #39

*Two characters clash because of their cultural backgrounds.*

**Ideas you can use:**

Do they have different values because of their religious faiths, their social class, or their family traditions?

Do they simply see things differently? Or is there an element of prejudice involved?

# MID-NOVEL WRITING PROMPT
## #40

*The MC discovers a resource she didn't know she had, just when she needs it most.*

**Ideas you can use:**

Does she find an inner strength or level of resilience? Maybe she's better at something than she thought she was, remembers a long-forgotten skill, or discovers a natural talent. What if she owns materials or tools she had thought useless junk until now, and one of the other characters recognises them for what they are?

To keep this plausible, don't make the step from discovery to solution too easy.

# MID-NOVEL WRITING PROMPT
## #41

*The MC gains an unexpected ally.*

**Ideas you can use:**

This could be a new person, or a character already established as part of the story. Is it someone who was previously opposed to the MC or her cause? Did she believe this person to be neutral or indifferent? Is one of the villain's minions defecting to her side?

Why does this person join the MC's cause now? What happened to change his mind? Has he, or someone dear to him, become a victim of the opposition? What if the villain treated his supporters badly, and one of them defects to the MC, bringing with him insider information?

What if the character was secretly on her side all along, supporting her quietly, and she is discovering this only now?

# MID-NOVEL WRITING PROMPT
## #42

*A stain provides information.*

**Ideas you can use:**

The information could simply be a clue to a character's personality or to a place's neglect, such as a food stain on a shirt, or mouldy water stains on the ceiling.

However, it could also provide a significant clue that takes the plot forward: the pattern of blood spatters on the wall, the spillage of soapy water where a character knocked over a bucket during his hasty escape.

The MC may observe the stain and draw her conclusions. Alternatively, she may have caused the stain herself. What if she has dinner with her prospective in-laws, knocks over her glass, and watches the red wine spread on the pristine white tablecloth? What if she discovers a tomato stain on the front of her blouse, the moment she enters the room for that crucial job interview?

# MID-NOVEL WRITING PROMPT
## #43

*A character needs to show identity papers—but either he doesn't have them, or they don't confirm the identity he claims.*

**Ideas you can use:**

What does he need to show: driving licence, passport, proof of age, certificate of good health, residence permission, membership card?

Why does he not have them? Has he forgotten or mislaid them? Have they been stolen? What does he do?

Are the papers forged, or do they belong to someone else? What happens when the discrepancy is detected?

Use this to cause delays or complications to the scene's plot.

# MID-NOVEL WRITING PROMPT
## #44

*The MC aims to convey a certain image of herself. How? Why?*

**Ideas you can use:**

Why? Does she want to impress someone? Is she trying to fit in with a crowd? Is she working on a personal brand for her freelance business?

How? Does she choose her clothes to suit the image? Does she behave in a certain way? Does she talk slang or jargon?

Does it work?

# MID-NOVEL WRITING PROMPT
## #45

*One person maligns another, but this actually makes that person appear more interesting. Or the opposite: one person praises another, but this makes other people respect the praised person less.*

**Ideas you can use:**

Who has an interest in either maligning or praising another person? What is his motivation?

Why does it have the opposite results than intended?

Perhaps the mother warns her teenage daughter that a certain boy has a bad reputation and must be avoided. This makes the bad boy all the more attractive to the girl.

What if a character assures the homicide detectives repeatedly that her lover is a noble, non-violent model citizen, who has never spoken a harsh word, let alone raised a hand against anyone? This is bound to raise red flags.

# MID-NOVEL WRITING PROMPT
## #46

*The MC is asked to provide a testimonial. He is biased.*

**Ideas you can use:**

What kind of testimonial? A reference for a former employee? An online book review? A safety certificate for a new product?

Is it a formal written testimonial, or simply a question that crops up during a conversation?

Why is he biased? What if he is in love with the person he's supposed to assess? What if the author, manufacturer, inventor or seller of the product is his close friend? What if it's someone he hates, or a business rival? What if he is being bribed or blackmailed to give a positive review/assessment/reference?

What does he do? Does he refuse to provide the testimonial? Does he place loyalty over honesty, and write a safety certificate for a faulty product, a glowing review for a poorly-written book? Or does he stay honest and give the product or book the low rating it deserves, although this will hurt the friend? Does he maintain his integrity and decline to get involved because of his bias? Does he take the bribe because he needs the cash?

# MID-NOVEL WRITING PROMPT
## #47

*The MC is waiting for something or someone.*

**Ideas you can use:**

Who or what is he waiting for? What has caused the delay?

What does he do while he is waiting? How does he feel? Is someone with him?

You can use the MC's wait to build suspense.

# MID-NOVEL WRITING PROMPT
## #48

*A character's purchase reveals something he'd rather not have known.*

### Ideas you can use:

What if someone sees him in a shop? What if the contents of his shopping trolley, or the item he pays for at the checkout, contradicts a claim he has made about himself and his lifestyle?

Perhaps he claimed to be a non-smoker, and is seen buying cigarettes. Maybe he says he's unmarried and living alone, and his shopping trolley contains tampons and diapers.

The purchase could be discovered later. Perhaps his wife notices a strange item on the credit card statement, or finds a bottle of perfume—a fragrance she would never wear—in his briefcase.

Does he offer excuses about why he bought this item? Are they convincing?

Maybe it's not what he bought, but when and where he made the purchase that gets him into trouble. Perhaps he's a suspect with a watertight alibi that proves he was out of town on the day of the murder... until a saleswoman remembers him, and the cash till and CCTV back this up.

# MID-NOVEL WRITING PROMPT
## #49

*A character wears an outfit that's very different from what he normally wears—not his style at all.*

**Ideas you can use:**

Why does he wear the different clothes? Is he trying out a new style? Has he come into money? Does he want to impress someone? Has he dressed for a specific occasion?

How do the people who know him react? Do they pretend not to notice, or do they tease him? Does someone make a sarcastic remark to his face or behind his back?

# MID-NOVEL WRITING PROMPT
## #50

*The MC loses his way.*

**Ideas you can use:**

Where does he get lost—on the road, in a strange town, in an apartment block, in a big hospital?

How did this happen—did he take the wrong turn, misread the map, get out of the lift on the wrong floor? Did he not pay enough attention because something or someone distracted him? Perhaps the satnav failed, or the instructions were inadequate.

What happens because of his error? Does he walk into the wrong room? Does he arrive late for an important appointment? Does he discover something he might not otherwise have seen? Does he meet someone who tells him the truth about the person he's come to meet?

# MID-NOVEL WRITING PROMPT
## #51

*The MC gets a pleasant surprise—something she would have thought highly unlikely.*

**Ideas you can use:**

Maybe she bungled the job interview... but gets an email offering her the job anyway. Perhaps the gallery owner rejected his exhibition entry... but a week later calls to say she wants his paintings after all. What if he thought he had only £5 in his wallet, but finds he has £50. What if he needs a specific product that hasn't been manufactured for thirty years... and his neighbour asks if he perchance wants that thing that's been cluttering up her garden shed, and it's exactly the right model and size.

# MID-NOVEL WRITING PROMPT
## #52

*A character insults the MC's competence, courage, looks or integrity.*

**Ideas you can use:**

What is the insult?

Why does the person make this remark?

Is the insult deliberate or unintentional?

Why does the MC feel insulted?

How does the MC react?

# MID-NOVEL WRITING PROMPT
## #53

*A character doesn't show enough grit/less grit than expected.*

### Ideas you can use:

In what way doesn't she show enough grit? Is she giving up a plan when she encounters an obstacle? Does she not have the self-discipline to see a project through when things get unpleasant? Does she succumb to bullying or discrimination?

Why does she lack grit? Is she generally weak-willed? Is she spoiled, used to easy victories, or accustomed to things going her way, and surprised to encounter resistance? Or does the situation demand something particularly repugnant of her?

What if she is normally strong with plenty of grit, but her willpower and resilience been weakened by recent events? Is she not her usual strong gritty self?

What if she doesn't truly lack grit, but only pretends to? Perhaps she has changed her mind about the project on ethical grounds. Perhaps her conscience won't let her get continue. What if she pretends to be a weak coward to get out of a commitment?

By showing not enough grit, is he letting someone down? Whom - her lover, her team mates, her fellow conspirators?

# MID-NOVEL WRITING PROMPT
## #54

*A character finds a valuable item in an unexpected place.*

**Ideas you can use:**

What does she find: money? Jewellery? A treasure map?

Where does she find it? In the rubbish bin, in a box of soap powder, in a pile of junk mail, in her cat's litter tray?

Who put it there, and why?

How does she come to stumble across it?

What will she do with it?

# MID-NOVEL WRITING PROMPT
## #55

*The MC has to endure something she dislikes.*

**Ideas you can use:**

What is it? A long journey with an obnoxious man sitting next to her on the bus? Painful treatment in a makeshift field hospital? Extreme discomfort in a hiding place? A two-hour sermon in an unheated church? Wet clothes?

Why does she have to endure it? Could she end this? If she has a choice, why doesn't she?

# MID-NOVEL WRITING PROMPT
## #56

*A character's hopes are dashed, but he will try again.*

**Ideas you can use:**

What did the character hope for? Who or what dashed his hopes?

How did he realise that his hopes had come to nothing—did some tell him, or did he see the results with his own eyes?

Why will he try again—because he must or because he wants to? Will he change his approach for the next attempt?

# MID-NOVEL WRITING PROMPT
## #57

*Everyone had expected this character to give up. To their surprise, he rallies new resources and shows hidden strength.*

**Ideas you can use:**

What did people think he would give up? His entry in a talent contest, his career ambitions, his pursuit of a girl, his art, his university studies, his scholarship application, his campaign to save the badger habitat?

Why did they expect him to give up? Did they see him as a loser type, or was the opposition too strong for him to have a chance? Had he talked about giving up? Was his scheme too hare-brained for anyone to take seriously?

Why does he go on? What new resources, approaches, inner strengths does he bring into play?

# MID-NOVEL WRITING PROMPT
# #58

*A character is reluctant to trust another.*

**Ideas you can use:**

Who distrusts whom? Why?

Is one of the characters the MC?

Is the distrust about a specific issue—such as money, company secrets, marital fidelity—or general?

Part of the character wants to trust the other person. Why does she want to (or need to) trust? Why can't she?

Is the distrust mutual?

How could you show the other person's trust or distrust?

# MID-NOVEL WRITING PROMPT
# #59

*A character demands an answer.*

**Ideas you can use:**

What if a wife demands the truth about her husband's financial commitments or about the nature of his relationship with a female friend?

What if a boss is suspicious about his employee's report and asks probing questions?

What if a police officer insists on details about the alibi?

Why does the character not want to give the answer—or not the full answer? What stops him from telling the whole truth?

How does the character avoid giving the answer? Does he try to change the subject, does he ask questions back, does he act insulted, does he tell a lie?

# MID-NOVEL WRITING PROMPT
## #60

*Characters play a game.*

**Ideas you can use:**

What kind of game is it? A card game, a board game, a paintball battle in the woods?

Who is playing? Friends, rivals, strangers?

Why do they play? To kill time, to measure their skills, to defeat the other, to win a championship?

Do they play purely for entertainment or is it a game for stakes? If the latter, what is at stake?

Who suggested the game?

Who is good at it?

How do the individuals feel about the game? Are they thrilled or bored? What if one is thrilled, the other bored?

Is one of the players cheating?

# MID-NOVEL WRITING PROMPT
# #61

*A character tidies and cleans the place.*

**Ideas you can use:**

Why does he clean up? To make a good impression? To avoid embarrassment? To hide evidence?

Is he expecting guests? Is an important client coming? Maybe he wants his abode to look nice for the lady he hopes will spend the night? Is he the hired weekly cleaner? Is he a teenager who has to show a tidy bedroom before he gets his parents' permission for something he wants? Is he a hygiene-obsessed cleaning freak with OCD?

Does he do the cleaning before other people arrive, or in their presence?

What exactly does he clean? Just the room where the meeting takes place? The food preparation area? The area vandalised by his jealous ex-wife?

# MID-NOVEL WRITING PROMPT
## #62

*A character expects an important visitor.*

**Ideas you can use:**

Whom does she expect? A client for her freelance business? A member of the Royal Family staying for the weekend? The man she loves in secret? A health and safety inspector?

How does she prepare? Order a takeaway meal, declutter the office, hire a cleaning service to overhaul the place, borrow furniture from a friend, wear her prettiest frock, spend hours doing and redoing her make-up, warn all her friends to stay away?

# MID-NOVEL WRITING PROMPT
## #63

*A child takes a sudden extreme dislike to an adult.*

**Ideas you can use:**

The reason for the child's reaction could be simple—perhaps she simply hates the mustard colour of that lady's dress. Maybe the adult has done something only the child finds terrible, such as rationed her intake of sweets (American: candy), or taken away the stuffed toy that has become a hygiene hazard.

However, the child's dislike could have sinister causes. Perhaps the uncle abused her sexually, or she witnessed the man commit a murder and is scared to speak up.

How does the child's dislike show? Focus especially on body language.

How do other adults respond? Do they react with alarm, or do they chide her? Do they take any notice at all?

What if the child's dislike is directed against the MC, and the child's parents assume the worst about him, just when it's crucial for him to gain the parents' trust?

# MID-NOVEL WRITING PROMPT
## #64

*The MC gets a new responsibility for which he isn't ready.*

### Ideas you can use.

Does he suddenly have custody of a child? Has he acquired a pet without intending to? Has he been promoted at work? Does he have to look after someone's garden, and no clue about what gardening involves? Did he accept a freelance assignment because he needed the money, and realised belatedly that it was way beyond his scope?

How does he respond to the announcement that the job is his? Does he shoulder the responsibility? Willingly or reluctantly? How does he feel about it? How does he cope? How seriously does he take it? What sacrifices does he make (voluntarily or involuntarily) to meet this obligation?

# MID-NOVEL WRITING PROMPT
## #65

*A character makes a ridiculous claim.*

**Ideas you can use:**

What is the claim? Who makes it? Why is it ridiculous? How do people react?

Perhaps nobody believes the claim. What if someone believes the claim, and this belief causes trouble for the MC?

Perhaps the claim isn't really ridiculous—but another character ridicules it, because she wants to discredit the witness.

# MID-NOVEL WRITING PROMPT
## #66

*A character observes something apparently supernatural.*

### Ideas you can use:

Who sees what? Is it visible, or is it a sound, a sensation, or other experience? What does he believe it is—a ghost, a divine message, a curse from the past?

How does he react? Whom does he tell about it?

What is the true cause of the phenomenon?

What if it really is supernatural?

# MID-NOVEL WRITING PROMPT
## #67

*Something the MC thought he had achieved is taken away from him.*

**Ideas you can use:**

Perhaps he wins a race, and afterwards gets disqualified on a technicality. Maybe the job promotion he was promised goes to someone else.

Is this change fair or unfair? How does he feel about it? Was he deliberately misled by someone, or had he deceived himself? Was he too hasty in celebrating before the results were confirmed?

What if someone manipulated the results? What if a rival influenced, bribed or blackmailed the decision-maker to revoke the earlier decree?

# MID-NOVEL WRITING PROMPT
## #68

*The MC receives an ominous warning.*

**Ideas you can use:**

What is the warning about?

How does it arrive? Does someone warn him during a conversation? Does it come by telephone, by email, or in an anonymous letter?

Does he heed it or laugh it off?

How does this warning relate to his plans in the current scene, or to the novel's overall plot?

Who sent the warning? Does the MC know from whom the warning came? Does he try to find out?

# MID-NOVEL WRITING PROMPT
# #69

*An item has vanished from the place where it was displayed for years.*

**Ideas you can use:**

What has vanished: an heirloom antique, a building, a wildlife preservation area, a statue, a sign 'whites only', a framed photograph?

What does the change signify? It can indicate how much time has passed, how society's attitudes have changed, that a political or environmental campaign has been won or lost, that new people now own the garden or manage the business.

It can signal a stage of personal growth: perhaps the child puts away the dolls she used to play with, or the widower takes down the framed portrait of his late wife because he is finally ready to start a new relationship.

It could also be a signal to the public: The dictator has been ousted from power, so his statue gets removed. A character may remove a framed membership certificate to demonstrate that he is no longer affiliated with that organisation.

The disappearance could also represent the loss. Perhaps the lawyer's licence has been revoked, and he no longer displays it. Perhaps she clung to the hope that her ex-husband would return to her, but when he marries someone else, she takes off her wedding ring.

What if the item has been stolen? What if its disappearance is a mystery? What if it is a clue to a crime?

# MID-NOVEL WRITING PROMPT
## #70

*The MC receives information she would have needed in a previous scene.*

**Ideas you can use:**

Why does this information arrive now? Had she tried to obtain this information before, and failed? Or is the content a complete surprise she never suspected?

How does she receive the information? Does someone tell her in a conversation, or send an email? Does she stumble across it while browsing the web or reading a newspaper?

How does she react?

In what way does this new information affect her plans and actions?

# MID-NOVEL WRITING PROMPT
# #71

*A character reacts differently than expected to news.*

**Ideas you can use:**

What is the news?

Who breaks it, and how?

How did the bearer of the message (or other people) expect this character to respond? Why?

How does she really react? What does she say? What's her body language? Describe her facial expression, her tone of voice, any pauses and hesitations in her reply. What does she do immediately after receiving the news? Does she take rapid action, or continue with what she was doing before, as if nothing had happened?

# MID-NOVEL WRITING PROMPT
## #72

The MC has to tell another character something unpleasant.

**Ideas you can use:**

What is this unpleasant information: that the character's husband has died in an accident, that her son has been arrested, that she has cancer, that her boyfriend is cheating her, that she failed the exam or that she didn't get the job?

Perhaps the MC is embarrassed to tell her that she has body odour or is dressed wrongly for the occasion.

What if the MC tells his girlfriend that they have no future and it's time to break up? What if he belatedly musters the courage to tell his fiancée that he already has a wife?

How long does the MC wait before speaking? Does he prepare, procrastinate, rehearse? Does he make several attempts without managing to come out with it? Or does he simply state it, without difficulty?

Is he trained or experienced in delivering this kind of message? For example, a police officer, social worker or doctor probably knows how to break bad news gently.

Does the MC do or say something to soften the blow?

How does the other character react? Pay attention to their body language.

# MID-NOVEL WRITING PROMPT
# #73

## *The MC encounters a religious object.*

**Ideas you can use:**

What is it? Where, how and why does he see it?

Does the item belong to the MC's own faith, or to a different religion?

Is it on display (such as a painted icon), or is another character using it (for example, counting the rosary beads).

Maybe a member of the expedition team clutches the medallion of St. Christopher, who for a long time was revered as the patron saint of travellers, when the ship is in danger of sinking. Perhaps the MC discovers that his girlfriend, who always claimed to be Jewish, is secretly praying to the Hindu goddess Parvati.

Is it an old artefact or a modern object? Is it used openly or in secret?

How does the MC feel about the item and about the religion?

# MID-NOVEL WRITING PROMPT
## #74

*A poster, wall plaque or information board contains a clue.*

**Ideas you can use:**

What is the clue? Where and how is it displayed?

Is the MC actively searching for the information when he reads the board, or is he looking for something else and suddenly sees the clue?

To make this incident interesting for your readers, consider making this an indirect clue rather than something obvious. The MC doesn't simply gain the insight by reading the display but by interpreting it in a different context.

# MID-NOVEL WRITING PROMPT
## #75

*The MC learns something about a person he thought he knew well.*

**Ideas you can use:**

Who is this person—a relative, a lover, a member of the team, a rival or the arch enemy? Is the person present in the scene, or absent?

What does he learn? How does he find this out—from the person herself or from a different source?

Why does this surprise him?

How does he feel about the revelation?

How does the person feel about the MC knowing this new information?

# MID-NOVEL WRITING PROMPT
## #76

*A character wants something, but hides her desire.*

**Ideas you can use:**

For this prompt, you can write about the MC or another character.

What does she want? Food? The man on whom she has a secret crush? A job promotion? A cat? A jewel hoard? A sports trophy? Appreciation?

Why does she hide her desire, and from whom? What would happen if her desire was discovered?

Does she pretend to be uninterested, or does she fake dislike? How does she do this?

Does anyone suspect?

# MID-NOVEL WRITING PROMPT
## #77

*The MC finds an item from his childhood.*

**Ideas you can use:**

What is it? A teddy bear, a photo, a letter, a toy he thought was long lost, a vase his mother treasured, a blanket from his grandparents' home?

Where does it find it? Is searching for it, or does he come across it by accident?

Why does this item turn up now?

What emotional associations does this item bring? Happy memories of cosy afternoons? Childhood bullying? Grief? Shame?

# MID-NOVEL WRITING PROMPT
# #78

*A character receives, presents or discovers a bunch of flowers.*

**Ideas you can use:**

Is the bouquet an expected ritual or a surprise?

Is it a gift to the hostess on visiting her home, or to the patient who's laid up in hospital? Does it represent an apology? If yes, for what?

Maybe a mystery admirer sends a bouquet with a floral delivery service or a ballerina receives flowers at the end of the show.

If you write a wedding scene, you may want to include the custom of the bride throwing her bouquet, with the assumption that whoever catches it will be the next bride.

How about flowers at a funeral, on a grave, or at the site of a fatal accident?

Maybe a character has preserved a bunch of flowers given to her long ago—at her first ball perhaps, or on occasion of her engagement, or by a suitor she loved but whom her parents rejected.

Are the flowers fresh or wilted? Shop-bought orchids, cosmos from the giver's garden, or wild violets picked in a forest clearing?

Does the recipient appreciate the flowers, treat them with disdain, or view them as a hypocritical gesture?

# MID-NOVEL WRITING PROMPT
## #79

*The MC realises something about herself.*

**Ideas you can use:**

What strength, weakness, or character flaw does she discover? Why has she not acknowledged this part of herself before?

What triggers the insight?

In what way does this self-knowledge affect what she does in this scene, and the choices she will make later in the novel?

# MID-NOVEL WRITING PROMPT
## #80

*A character's loyalties are questioned.*

**Ideas you can use:**

For this prompt, you can write about the MC or a different character.

Who questions his loyalties—he himself, because he is no longer certain that a person or cause deserves his loyalty? Or someone else—his boss, his superior officer, his wife?

What if the MC has suspicions about a team member's loyalty? What if the team leader thinks the MC is disloyal? Are the suspicions justified?

What causes examination of loyalties? What incident has put them in question?

How does he respond?

# MID-NOVEL WRITING PROMPT
# #81

*The MC has a health problem or injury.*


**Ideas you can use:**

This can be a chronic problem that flares up at the worst possible moment, such as osteoarthritis in the knee just when he needs to jump from the window onto the road. Or it could be an acute injury, like a sprained ankle.

Perhaps the problem is the result of his actions in the previous scenes. What if the recent stress and lack of sleep give him a pounding headache? What if he spent so much time searching information on the computer that he now has severe eye strain?

Maybe he caught an infectious illness from people with whom he spent time in a previous scene. How about a wound that refuses to heal, sustained in a duel or brawl?

How does this illness or injury impact his actions? Does he need to take time out? Is he laid up in hospital? Is he unable to concentrate on the task at hand and misses a crucial clue?

How does he react to the handicap? Does he pretend it doesn't exist, or use it as an excuse to get out of an unwanted duty? When talking about it to others, does he play it up or down?

# MID-NOVEL WRITING PROMPT
## #82

*The MC resolves to improve his fitness.*

**Ideas you can use:**

Why? What triggers his resolution? Does he want to overcome or prevent a health problem? Has his doctor or his wife urged him? Does he want to impress ladies, or one lady in particular? Is he scared of ageing? Does he need to pass a fitness test to access a career path? Did a recent experience cause him a shock about how unfit he has become?

Does he actually act on his resolution, or does he only think about it and postpone the action?

What steps (if any) does he take immediately? Does he go for a run, sign up for a gym membership, hire a personal trainer, buy an instruction DVD?

What kind of fitness programme does he join/do/think about? Martial arts? Yoga? Circuit training? Weight lifting?

Does he tell anyone about his resolution? If yes, whom?

# MID-NOVEL WRITING PROMPT
## #83

*The MC spontaneously visits a place where he has never been before.*

**Ideas you can use:**

What place does he visit? The home of someone he's neglected or avoided? A museum, library, art gallery? A gym? A recruitment centre?

What motivates him? Curiosity? Personal challenge? Professional duty?

# MID-NOVEL WRITING PROMPT
## #84

*A character contradicts the MC.*

**Ideas you can use:**

What exactly does the MC say?

How does the other person contradict him? Why?

Who is present?

Who is right—the MC, the other person, or both in different ways?

How does the MC react?

# MID-NOVEL WRITING PROMPT
## #85

*A sound or smell reminds the MC of something.*

**Ideas you can use:**

What is this smell, and what does it remind her of?

Could it be a smell from her childhood, a song on the radio that she used to dance to with her first boyfriend, a perfume she used to love?

# MID-NOVEL WRITING PROMPT
## #86

*There's a problem with a lock or a key.*

**Ideas you can use:**

What needs to be locked or unlocked? A cash box, a filing cabinet, a jewellery box, the front door, a suitcase, a car, the way out?

Is the key lost or broken? Is the door jammed? Is there a key sticking in the lock from the other side of the door? Has the lock been changed?

What problems does this cause for whom?

# MID-NOVEL WRITING PROMPT
## #87

*Interesting prints on a surface convey information.*

**Ideas you can use:**

How about footprints, paw prints, tyre marks, or fingerprints?

# MID-NOVEL WRITING PROMPT
## #88

*A character doesn't have time to do what needs doing.*

**Ideas you can use:**

Why is he in such a hurry? Is he on a more urgent mission? Does he have an important appointment to keep? Does he not want to miss a rare chance to see a famous star perform, or to meet the girl on whom he has a crush?

What does he do about the task he's not doing? Does he ignore it, postpone it, tell someone else to do it?

# MID-NOVEL WRITING PROMPT
## #89

*A character conveys a message through a work of art.*

**Ideas you can use:**

What kind of art is it? A painting, a musical composition, a statue, a poem, a dance?

What does it express? An emotion, an accusation, coded information, a clue to whodunit?

For whom is the message intended? Does that person immediately understand what it says?

# MID-NOVEL WRITING PROMPT
## #90

*A character calls in a favour from the MC.*

**Ideas you can use:**

What kind of favour does this person ask?

Is the MC happy or reluctant to grant this favour? Does she do it?

Why does the MC owe this person a favour?

# MID-NOVEL WRITING PROMPT
## #91

*A noise intrudes into the current scene.*

**Ideas you can use:**

What kind of noise: Building work, loud music from the flat (American: apartment) above, a beeping phone, a shrilling doorbell, the rumblings of an earthquake?

How do the characters respond?

# MID-NOVEL WRITING PROMPT
## #92

*A character declares an ambition which takes the MC by surprise.*

**Ideas you can use:**

What is this person's goal? Does he want to go back to school, marry an heiress, win a sports championship?

Why does this surprise the MC?

# MID-NOVEL WRITING PROMPT
## #93

*The MC discovers that he has something in common with the antagonist.*

**Ideas you can use:**

The antagonist can be the MC's rival, an enemy, a criminal or an evil villain.

What do they have in common? Did they grow up in the same orphanage or have the same teacher? Do they share the same hobby or taste in music? Do they pursue the same ambition? Do they hold the same values deep down? Are they in love with the same woman?

How does the MC discover this similarity?

# MID-NOVEL WRITING PROMPT
# #94

*A liquid spills, causing complications.*

**Ideas you can use:**

The spillage can be minute or monumental.

What if someone spills a drink over another person's dress? What if a waterpipe bursts, disrupting proceedings? Perhaps a dam bursts and the settlement must be evacuated. Could there be a petrol spillage on the motorway, forcing everyone to drive slowly? Perhaps a tanker has dumped illegal chemical waste into the sea, causing environmental devastation.

How do the characters become aware of this spillage? How do they react?

In what way does this affect the events in the scene?

# MID-NOVEL WRITING PROMPT
# #95

*A character doesn't turn up.*

**Ideas you can use:**

Who is waiting for him, where and why?

Why doesn't he come? Did he forget the appointment, did he change his mind, did he defect to the enemy or has he been murdered?

Where is he supposed to arrive? What do the other characters do while they are waiting? Show them getting increasingly impatient, worried or angry.

# MID-NOVEL WRITING PROMPT
## #96

*A character tries to rectify an earlier mistake.*

**Ideas you can use:**

You can write about the MC or another character for this prompt.

What mistake did she make? When did she realise that this was a mistake?

Does she attempt to undo the mistake, to hide it, or to limit the damage? How?

How successful is she with this attempt?

# MID-NOVEL WRITING PROMPT
## #97

*A character receives a gift.*

**Ideas you can use:**

From whom is the gift? On what occasion? What is it?

Is this gift expected or a surprise? Is it socially acceptable?

Is it wrapped? Does the giver present this in person, or send it by post, or leave it anonymously on the doorstep?

How does the recipient feel about this gift? Is she pleased? Embarrassed? Annoyed? Alarmed?

Who else is present when she receives the gift?

# MID-NOVEL WRITING PROMPT
## #98

### *The MC is tired.*

**Ideas you can use:**

Why is he tired? Has he had too little sleep recently? Did he stay up late last night? Have the events of the past few days tired him? Is he mentally drained from continued concentration, or physically exhausted from a hard labour?

Can he go to sleep, take a nap, rest for a while? If not, why not?

# MID-NOVEL WRITING PROMPT
# #99

*MC eats food she's never thought of eating.*

**Ideas you can use:**

What is she eating? Why?

What if the meal looks revolting, but she doesn't wish to offend the hostess or the cook?

Is she travelling in a part of the world where restaurants serve exotic foods—perhaps even dishes she finds repulsive. How about raw dog stomach (a speciality of northern China), wok-fried cat (common in southern China), snails (a delicacy in France), rat, monkey, termites?

Is she in a survival situation where this strange stuff is the only available nourishment?

Perhaps she is simply curious and wants to try something different. Or maybe she is acting on a dare. ("I dare you to eat this frog alive.")

What if the food is obtained through extreme cruelty to animals— foie gras, frogs' legs, shark fins, lobster slowly boiled alive—and she cannot bear to think of the creatures' suffering? In this case, what makes her eat the dish anyway?

How difficult is it for her to overcome her revulsion (if that's what she feels)? Does she pretend pleasure? How?

Maybe she thinks the food is delicious. In this case, describe the flavours and textures so the reader can share the culinary joy.

Are other people sharing the meal? How are they enjoying it?

# MID-NOVEL WRITING PROMPT
# #100

*The MC changes his tactics.*

**Ideas you can use:**

What were his tactics until now?

Why does he change his approach? The old way probably didn't work. When and how did he realise this?

Is he acting on new intelligence received?

What will his new tactics be?

# DEAR READER,

I hope you found these ideas helpful and that they have added exciting twists to your story.

I'd love it if you could post a review on Amazon or some other book site where you have an account and posting privileges. Maybe you can mention what kind of fiction you write, and explain which chapters you found most helpful and why.

Email me the link to your review, and I'll send you a free review copy (ebook) of one of my other Writer's Craft books. Let me know which one you would like: *Writing Fight Scenes, Writing Scary Scenes, The Word-Loss Diet, Writing About Magic, Writing About Villains, Writing Dark Stories, Euphonics For Writers, Writing Short Stories to Promote Your Novels, Twitter for Writers, Why Does My Book Not Sell? 20 Simple Fixes, Writing Vivid Settings, How To Train Your Cat To Promote Your Book, Writing Deep Point of View, Getting Book Reviews, Novel Revision Prompts, Writing Vivid Dialogue, Writing Vivid Characters, Writing Book Blurbs and Synopses, Writing Vivid Plots, Writing Vivid Emotions, Write Your Way Out Of Depression: Practical Self-Therapy For Creative Writers.*

My email is contact@raynehall.com. Also drop me a line if you've spotted any typos which have escaped the proofreader's eagle eyes, or want to give me private feedback or have questions.

You can also contact me on Twitter: https://twitter.com/RayneHall. Tweet me that you've read this book, and I'll probably follow you back.

If you find this book helpful, it would be great if you could spread the word about it. Maybe you know other writers who would benefit.

I'm also adding an excerpt from another Writer's Craft Guide you may find useful: *Writing Vivid Plots.* I hope you like it.

With best wishes for your novel-in-progress,

Rayne Hall

# ACKNOWLEDGEMENTS

I give sincere thanks to the beta readers and critiquers who read the draft chapters and offered valuable feedback: Douglas Kolacki, Philip T. Stephens, Larisa Walk.

The book cover is by Erica Syverson and Uros Jovanovic. Julia Gibbs proofread the manuscript, and Bogdan Matei formatted the book.

And finally, I say thank you to my sweet cat Sulu who snuggled on the desk between my arms with his paw on my wrist and purred his approval as I typed. He particularly likes the prompts involving animals and recommends featuring a black rescue cat.

Rayne Hall

# EXCERPT: WRITING VIVID PLOTS

## INTRODUCTION

Do you want to give your novel a powerful story line? Do you want to power up a draft you've written?

This guide shows professional techniques for developing and structuring your fiction.

In the first four chapters, I'll present four plotting methods to choose from: the Hero's Journey model, the Three-Act structure, the Goal-and-Obstacles approach and the Character Arc story. You don't need to adhere to them slavishly. Rather, I recommend that you take them, play with them and change them so they suit the story you want to write.

You can take two or more methods and layer them. You'll find that in many places the layers click together like they're variants of the same concept. Elsewhere they may contradict each other, and in this case, you simply make an artistic choice.

This book shows solutions to plot problems such as slow beginnings, sagging middles and flat endings, and guides you to write specific story parts such as the 'Black Moment' and the 'Climax'.

The focus of this guide is on plotting full-length novels, but there are also chapters on plotting short stories, series and serials.

If you're new to the writer's craft, you may find this book too advanced, and I suggest you start with a basic fiction writing guide. If you're an experienced author, you'll inevitably be familiar with some of the concepts I present. Treat those chapters as refreshers for what you already know.

I use British English, which may look strange if you're used to American word choices, grammar, punctuation and spelling, but I'm confident that you can follow the text. To avoid clunky 'he or she' and 'him or her' constructions, I switch between male and female pronouns. Everything in this book applies to either gender.

Now let's get to work.

Rayne

## CHAPTER 1: PLOTTING WITH THE HERO'S JOURNEY

Some stories are millennia old and still popular—that surely makes them the most successful stories of all times. Joseph Campbell (1904-1987) identified what these stories have in common, and found that they share a similar plot structure.

The structure is called 'the Hero's Journey'.

As modern writers, we can use the same plot structure—modified of course, to suit our times, our fiction and our readers—to create the same kind of power.

Here are the main stages of the Hero's Journey. See if you can recognise them in your story, or if you could structure your next book with them.

### 1. THE ORDINARY WORLD

The main character (MC) is in her accustomed world. This is an opportunity to show her surroundings, her skills, her values and her personality. In modern novels, this section is often very short.

### 2. THE CALL TO ADVENTURE

A 'herald' arrives telling the 'hero' that he must go on a quest. This can be the boss sending him on a dangerous assignment, a client hiring the private investigator for a job, an email telling him that his little niece has disappeared, or a solicitor's letter informing him that he has inherited a farm in the middle of nowhere.

The 'Call to Adventure' combined with the 'Ordinary World' can form the first scene of the novel: show the MC at work, and then his boss gives him the scary assignment.


## 3. REFUSAL OF THE CALL

At first, the MC doesn't want to go and flat out refuses. She has good reasons to decline the assignment: she isn't qualified, she doesn't believe it's necessary, she's retired and doesn't want to get involved with police work again, or she promised her husband never again to take a job away from home.

But she soon learns that she must go. She's the only one who knows the location of the bunker, the only one with the special skill, the only one the evil villain agrees to receive. Perhaps she needs to complete this mission because she failed a previous one, and this is her only chance to save her career or to regain her self-respect. Maybe the problem is partly her fault, because she let the serial killer suspect go last year, and now he's slaughtered several more innocents, so she'll never forgive herself unless she brings him in. Maybe she didn't believe in the cause at first, but new events tell her this is a serious and worthwhile undertaking. Perhaps there's social pressure on her to go—if she refuses, she'll be branded as a coward, or her neighbours will think of her as the cop who refused to help rescue the abducted child.

So she accepts the assignment.

This refusal and acceptance of the call can happen in a few dialogue lines, or they can spread over several scenes.


## 4. MEETING THE MENTOR

The MC gets valuable advice from a knowledgeable, wise person. He may consult a subject expert, get a thorough briefing from his boss, seek advice from someone who's recently travelled in that country, meet up with a retired colleague, or seek out someone who has accomplished a similar quest.

Often, the mentor is reluctant to give advice. She doesn't think that the MC is experienced/skilled enough for the task and warns him not to undertake the suicidal venture, or she doesn't want to share her knowledge with someone of the wrong gender/wrong skin colour/ wrong tribal affiliations/wrong attitude. It's also possible that she has buried the knowledge deep in her memory and doesn't wish to have anything to do with those matters ever again.

This creates tension because the MC desperately needs the information. He must prove himself worthy of the mentor's guidance, or appeal to her loyalty or conscience to get her help.

## 5. PREPARING FOR THE JOURNEY

The MC gets ready for the adventure. Depending on the kind of quest, he may hastily snatch his service revolver and jump into the car, or he can devote weeks to careful planning and preparation.

Here are some things mythical heroes do to prepare. Adapt them for your story.

- The MC assembles a team/crew/task force to tackle the job/ go on the expedition/hunt the killer.

- The MC acquires a sidekick who'll go with him on the journey, whether the MC wants this companion or not.

- Visiting the armourer. The MC gets a special kind of weapon. Depending on the genre, this may be an actual weapon (a gun, a sword), a custom-made gadget or special equipment.

- He gets some magical, paranormal or spiritual item or blessing. Maybe a priest will bless the vessel on which he and his crew will sail, a witch gives him a potion to use in a specific kind of emergency, his father bestows on him his great-grandfather's courage-giving ring, a friend hangs a protective amulet around his neck, or the community presents him with a religious relic.

- Tearful parting from a loved one. The MC says goodbye to someone special. This can be a lover, a parent, a young child. The farewell is poignant because they don't want to part, and because they are aware they may never meet again. Perhaps the hero's beloved mother has cancer and may not be alive by the time he comes back. Maybe his wife is pregnant with their first child which he may not survive to see. Make this scene heart-wrenching.

## 6. CROSSING THE THRESHOLD

The MC needs to enter a new kind of world—another country, a new type of business—but she can't just walk in. There's a 'gatekeeper' who tries to stop her, for example, a ferocious dog attacking her at the entrance to the mansion, a receptionist who won't let her pass, or a manager who tells her she's not wanted in the department.

It's important that the MC doesn't show fear, and she doesn't employ violence against the gatekeeper or defeat him. Rather, she uses courage and wit to persuade him to let her through.

If possible, put an actual door or gateway into this scene to signify the crossing of the threshold.

## 7. LEARNING THE RULES OF THE NEW WORLD

Now the MC is in the new world, and he has to learn how everything works here. He may have to master the language, make sense of customs and rituals, understand taboos and grasp the hidden meanings of what is said.

Make the new world as different from the old as possible. Show the MC struggling, making mistakes, unwittingly causing offence, getting robbed or ripped off, learning and adapting.

This can be a single scene, or it may spread over several scenes. The learning of the rules can also take place in the 'Crossing the Threshold' scene or as part of the 'Trail of Trials'.

Surprisingly often, the first 'Learning the Rules' takes place in a tavern, pub, inn, bar or saloon. That's a natural choice. After all, if you were to travel to an unknown country to face untold dangers, you would probably spend a night in a hotel and get your bearings in a coffee shop too. It's the kind of place where strangers can learn about the new world before immersing themselves fully into that world—a sensible choice.

## 8. THE TRAIL OF TRIALS

In modern fiction, this section can spread over many chapters. Here are some events happening in myths at this stage. Adapt them to suit your novel.

- The MC gets tested.
- A duel.
- A tournament.
- The MC makes an enemy.
- The MC gains allies.
- After some problems, the team members learn to act together and trust one another.
- A new member joins the team.
- The MC proves himself a worthy leader of the team.
- The MC gets a new outfit/costume.
- The locals put the MC through some kind of aptitude test.
- The MC travels on a dangerous route.

## 9. APPROACH TO THE INNERMOST CAVE

The MC enters a danger zone—the vampire queen's castle, the lair of the wolves, the sadistic scientist's laboratory, the religious cult's secret initiation chamber. On the way there, the MC sees some spooky/ghastly/shocking things, perhaps evidence of abuse and cruelty. The deeper he gets, the more gruesome the sights. (The level of gruesomeness depends on the genre: Horror fiction may show dismembered bodies, Romance fiction won't.)

Consider an underground setting for this part of your novel—somewhere dark, deep in the earth, reached only after a long descent. How about a dungeon, a bunker, a canyon, a railway tunnel, an abandoned mineshaft, a storage cellar, the basement of a closed factory?

This is a section of slow pace and high suspense. Stretch it out, and keep the reader on the edge of her seat. If it suits your story, use sensory impressions to create a creepy atmosphere.


## 10. THE ORDEAL

This part often comes midway into the novel. The MC suffers physical, mental or emotional pain—or all three. Perhaps he got caught when he tried to infiltrate the villain's underground headquarters, and now the villain's henchmen apply torture to make him reveal his secrets.

Make this experience as painful and scary as your story and genre allow.

You can give the scene poignancy by making the suffering part voluntary. For example, the MC may suffer torture rather than reveal the secret, or he may allow himself to be abused in order to buy time for his friends to escape.

Sometimes the Approach to the Innermost Cave and the Ordeal are not physical actions but a descent into the dark part of the MC's own psyche.


## 11. THE INITIATION

This can be a positive or a negative event—but it is definitely an intense experience which transforms the MC somehow.

As part of the initiation, she may have to bring a major sacrifice or surrender herself in some way, and she may be granted something precious. She may become wiser, or be accepted into a secret society.

She may experience a form of death and rebirth, either symbolically or physically or both. Physically, this often means a near-fatal injury or a near-fatal event, perhaps the direct consequence of the ordeal, or an accident during her escape.

If your story allows, make your MC lose consciousness for a while. Perhaps she faints at the wonderful/terrible sight of something during the initiation, or she lost so much blood during the ordeal that she passed out, or she was nearly drowned during the shipwreck and when she comes to she's been washed onto a beach. She might also survive a murder attempt that leaves her comatose for days.

Whatever happens, when she regains her consciousness, physically and/or symbolically, she is changed. The transformation is crucial.

## 12. SEIZING THE PRIZE

The MC now takes something precious (a special sword, a magical elixir, the secret code, the abducted princess, evidence of the government minister's corruption) and carries it away with him. He probably found this special something in the innermost cave during the ordeal or initiation.

In many novels, this prize is what he set out to gain from the start.

## 13. THE ROAD BACK

Now that she has seized the prize, she takes it back to the 'ordinary world' where it is needed or where it belongs.

But the journey back is not smooth. To start with, the evil villain won't simply put up with the loss, but goes after the MC to get it back. At this stage, there is also often a betrayal, as one of the MC's team turns against her, or is revealed as an agent of the enemy.

*Mid-Novel Writing Prompts*

# 14. RESURRECTION

This section is the Climax (or a Climax) of the story. In some ways, it is similar to the 'Approach to the Innermost Cave—Ordeal—Initiation' sequence, but things happen much faster. You may have high speed action here.

There's often a confrontation with the villain, complete with physical fighting. If the MC has already defeated the villain earlier, then the villain comes back, set on getting revenge as well as on retrieving the prize. The MC may also realise that the baddie he defeated was just a lieutenant, and now he finds out who the real evil mastermind is, a twist which works great in Thrillers and Horror.

Again, the MC almost dies before he triumphs, and often a metaphorical or ritual purification takes place as the hero is 'resurrected'.

In some novels, the hero really dies at this stage. In this case, someone else (perhaps his sidekick, his lover or his team mates) takes up his spirit, completes the mission and brings the prize safely back into the Ordinary World.

The Climax can be action-based (e.g. in Fantasy) or emotional (e.g. in Romance) or a combination of both.


# 15. ARRIVAL BACK HOME

As the MC re-enters the ordinary world, she may meet that same gatekeeper again, which is a good opportunity to show how she has grown and changed.

She has to remember or even re-learn the once-familiar rules of the Ordinary World which now may strike her as petty or strange. She may settle comfortably into her old routines, or she may chafe at the restrictions and yearn for the freedom and adventure of her quest.

Do you want a happy ending, a tragic ending, or a bittersweet one? Here are your options.

How do people in the Ordinary World respond to the prize – with gratitude, awe or indifference? In some stories, they don't actually care for the prize the MC went to such great lengths to obtain. The police chief suppresses the evidence, the newspaper editor decides not to run the story, the king pours the elixir down his castle's garderobe (latrine) shaft.

If they value the prize, how do they treat the person who brought it? Do they hail her as a hero and elect her mayor of the community? Or do they imprison her, demote her, or chase her out of town? Maybe they kill her the moment she arrives, snatch the prize and misuse its power?

How does the reunion with the loved one go? Perhaps they have a tearful, happy meeting. But the old mother may have died just before the MC arrived back, and the lover for whom the MC undertook the quest and risked her life hasn't waited for her but married someone else.

## CREATIVE FREEDOM

In your novel, you may have all these parts or only some of them, and they don't necessarily happen in exactly this order. Even the ancient myths don't all use the structure as it is. It's quite flexible, so adapt it. Sometimes several of these stages happen simultaneously, or one may be much longer than all the others.

## PROFESSIONAL TIP

The Hero's Journey is great for revising individual parts of a complete novel draft. Instead of structuring your whole book with this model, pick a section which needs more drama and depth. Consider which of the stages of the Hero's Journey it might correspond to, and use this for inspiration.

## EXAMPLE

At the end of this book, I'll share the beginning of one of my books, the dark epic fantasy novel *Storm Dancer*, so you can see how I handled the 'Call to Adventure', 'Refusal of the Call' and 'Meeting the Mentor' stages.

## CHAPTER 2: THE THREE-ACT PLOT STRUCTURE

Each story (novel, short story, myth, screenplay) needs a beginning, a middle and an end. These three sections are 'acts':

- Act 1: Beginning
- Act 2: Middle
- Act 3: Ending

However, the three sections are not of equal length. Depending on the genre and the story you want to tell, the middle is probably longer than the beginning and the ending. In many modern novels, the beginning is very short.

Imagine a novel divided into six equal parts. The beginning accounts for just one of them, the middle for three, and the ending for two.

## ACT 1: THE BEGINNING

In this section, you need to establish the 'rules of the world', what kind of environment and society the main character lives in, and what kind of person he is, his strengths, weaknesses and ambitions. However, resist the temptation to explain to the reader what she needs to know. Instead, show the information subtly woven into dialogue and action.

An 'Inciting Incident' happens that upsets the status quo and propels the character into action.

If you layer the Three-Act plot structure with the Hero's Journey plot structure, the beginning typically contains the Ordinary World, the Call to Adventure, Resisting the Call, Meeting the Mentor and

Preparing for the Quest. Each of these points may span over a whole scene, but in modern novels, they often take only a few paragraphs each.

## THE CURTAIN BETWEEN ACT 1 and ACT 2

Between these two acts is a doorway the main character must open and walk through, or, if you prefer, a curtain to lift. This signifies the MC's conscious decision to enter a new world or new phase of life. He knows that once he has lifted this curtain, things will never be the same again.

This curtain corresponds with Crossing the Threshold in the Hero's Journey.

## ACT 2: THE MIDDLE

The protagonist experiences struggles and growth as she gathers clues and acts on them. The stakes get raised. This is roughly the equivalent of the Trail of Trials.

In the middle of Act 2 there's a Midpoint Reversal. This is the moment when everything turns upside down, and the MC changes direction. She may realise that she has sworn allegiance to the wrong person, or is about to marry the wrong man, or that the cause she devoted herself to is not noble, but evil. She changes course, adapting her goal or her strategy, or even using her skills to do exactly the opposite of what she has done up to now.

Shortly before or after the Midpoint Reversal, or at the same time, is the Black Moment when all seems lost. The MC is in the worst possible situation, perhaps imprisoned, injured, trapped and betrayed. She is close to giving up but rallies her courage.

In the Hero's Journey, these events happen during the Approach to the Innermost Cave, Ordeal and Resurrection.

## THE CURTAIN BETWEEN ACT 2 AND ACT 3

Once again, the MC decides to open a door and enter a new phase. This is often a heart-wrenching or dangerous decision.

## ACT 3: THE ENDING

The story reaches the Climax. This scene pitches the MC against the main antagonist, perhaps in a duel to the death between hero and villain or a confrontation between investigator and serial killer. The book's tension is at its highest.

Next comes the Resolution when the MC's problems are solved and the goal is achieved (or lost, depending on the kind of story you're writing) and problems are solved.

There may be a Denouement showing what happens after the main story is over. Sometimes this is in the form of an epilogue, a scene taking place some years later. For example, a Romance novel may give a glimpse of the couple's happy married life with their children, to reassure the reader that the two are indeed living happily ever after.

If you layer the Three-Act plot structure with the Hero's Journey, you may find that the elements don't match up exactly in the second half of your book. For example, the Climax may or may not correspond to the Resurrection, although the Resolution usually matches the Arrival Back Home.

## PROFESSIONAL TIP

Model the relative length of your acts on those of the bestsellers in your genre.

# CHAPTER 3: THE GOAL-AND-OBSTACLES PLOT STRUCTURE

The main character wants or needs to achieve something, works towards that goal, and will do anything to achieve it.

For example, the farmer fights to keep the property developers from his ancestors' lands, the homicide detective hunts the serial killer, the lawyer fights to prove her client's innocence, the archaeologist seeks the location of the ancient temple, the heiress wants to find true love.

The MC has compelling reasons to need this, and story events make it even more important that she succeeds. Raise the tension by raising the stakes continuously.

The plot consists of a series of obstacles preventing the MC's success, and the MC's actions to overcome them.

Typically, the MC makes three major attempts, each consisting of several steps.

## PART 1

The MC needs to achieve the goal. He sees the obstacles and confidently works to overcome them, using his skills, strengths and attitudes. But an unexpected obstacle arises, and he fails.

## PART 2

Something terrible happens that makes it even more important that the MC achieves his goal. He cannot afford to fail. The obstacles are bigger than before. Again using his skills, strengths and attitudes, he tries again. He even makes a sacrifice or pays a price to succeed. But he fails once more.

## PART 3

Dejected, the MC loses hope and is close to giving up. But something happens that infuses him with the courage of desperation. Perhaps it's a woman's love, perhaps it's the life of a child at stake, perhaps it's a memory of his late father. He realises that he must go on. He also realises that he has gone about it the wrong way, that the previous failures were in part his fault because he used the wrong approach or attitude. He changes something—perhaps himself.

## PART 4

He tries again, this time differently. If he previously used lies, he now uses honesty. If he previously used his authority, he now tries humility. This new attempt is more difficult and more dangerous than anything he's ever done, the obstacles seem insurmountable, and he is tempted to slide back into his familiar old ways, but he perseveres. He succeeds.

## PROFESSIONAL TIP

If you want to make this story tense and exciting, give it a 'Ticking Clock'—a deadline by when the goal must be achieved, or terrible consequences may happen.

For example, unless the detective finds the serial killer before the next full moon, he will kill another child, or unless the secret agent discovers and disables the trigger mechanism by that date, a nuclear bomb will destroy New York. This creates urgency and keeps the reader on the edge of her seat.

Made in the USA
Middletown, DE
23 February 2021